MW00653358

DON'T DIE

with Your Song Unsung

Gary Russo

Andrea T. Goeglein, PhD

SERVINGSUCCESS®

Contents

To my daughters Amber and Cara:
Thank you for teaching me how rich I am.

To Tracy:
Your courage encouraged me to find my real self.

Acknowledging All Those Who Helped Me Smile

The list of creative projects I wanted to pursue included writing a book. This book happened because my dear cousin Andrea Goeglein, who has been teaching me how the universe works, took my words and created a book. Thank you.

I am thankful for David Fischer, Damian, and Jennie for crossing my path when the time was right.

Geoff, Jan, Tony, and my friends from the Rockaway Artist Alliance: thank you for surrounding me with all of your talents. Most of all, thank you, Apryl, for your unlimited support.

Penelope, thank you for sharing your story and allowing me to rewrite my story. Thank you for seeing how blessed I was before I could. And my many thanks for helping me see what you saw in me.

I thank my brothers and sisters from Iron Workers Local 40 and 361 for your support and leadership in helping me build a little part of this great country. I wrote this book in part for all of the "hard hats" around the world.

Thank you, Willy, for always looking out for me.

I send special thanks to my fellow workers at the 2nd Avenue Subway site. Your help and friendship will never be forgotten. To Paul, Dan, Sean, Jay, Scott, Frank, and the Schiavone boys: we did it together.

Hank, Greg, Dave, Kenny, Wayne, and the entire Kiewit family: thank you for helping me learn how to be the best I can be.

I am grateful for my wonderful "neighborhood family" on 73rd Street and 2nd Avenue who made this happen.

I thank the Russo-Maturo-Parrino-Troiano clan for making me part of this strong, wonderful family.

Poppy and KK: thank you for helping in more ways than just the obvious.

And I thank the Gaffney and Battillo families for giving me my roots.

And lastly, I recognize what came first: I thank my parents (all four of you) for each giving me a piece of my puzzle.

Love to all,

10/6/11

To Love, Love of Family,
and the magic that occurs when
Forgiveness meets Synchronicity

Don't Die without Acknowledging Gratitude

I had the knowledge and experience, Gary Russo had the story, and Katherine Armstrong masterfully edited and merged all the pieces to create this book. Thank you, Katherine, for editing this book, for introducing me to the first *Don't Die*® editor, Deborah McKew, and for helping me to be a better writer. Your mark has been on the *Don't Die* series from the beginning, and I hope that it does not end with this book.

To all the Goeglein clan—Richard, Eric, Scott, Dana, Beth, LuLu, Kevin, Miles, Gage, and Gabby: Thank you for your patience as I turned our family reunion into a retrospective journey of my early life with Gary Russo.

And, of course, to my cousin Gary. The words of Linda Ellerbee express my gratitude the best:

We are seasoned in each other's lives, our joys and sorrows woven into the tapestry of shared history.

Thank you for living with a *Don't Die* spirit and your willingness to create a renewed history together.

Andrea
10/5/11

The world needs dreamers, the world needs doers. But most of all, the world needs dreamers who do.

—Sara Ban Breathnach

I did not set out to find myself or improve myself. I set out to make money, so I started reading books about setting goals and visualizing the end game. It was only when I set out to do what I loved—singing for others—with the only pay I thought about being the richness of people's smiles, that I really found what I was looking for. Myself.

—Gary Russo

Welcome

I opened the first *Don't Die* book with these words:

> *This book is my attempt to dispel a myth that has been*
> *perpetrated on the unsuspecting masses for many genera-*
> *tions. The myth I refer to is the one that assures if you do*
> *your homework, earn good grades, and graduate from the*
> *right schools, you will land a job or create a business that*
> *will provide you riches, happiness, health, and love; you will*
> *achieve your "happily ever after."*

The rest of the book was devoted to dispelling that myth and sharing a real story of how happily ever after really happens.

I continue *The Crooked Road of Success®*, *Don't Die* Small Books, Big Impact series with a true story* that is still unfolding as this book goes to press in October, 2011. This book will, yet again, disprove the myth of happily ever after, and share a story of creating life happiness so real that myths, however attractive, simply can't compete with the here and now.

As synchronicity would have it, Gary Russo, the construction-worker-turned-Sinatra-sensation who tells his story in

---

*All stories in this book are true. Some details have been changed to protect identities, streamline events, and give the reader a greater understanding of the events discussed.

this book, is my cousin. He shares insights, emails, and photos that capture the trajectory of his remarkable year. His goals are simply to sing. To make people smile. To use singing to make other people smile.

Gary's story animates these recognizable and universal personal development adages:

- Change your awareness and your perspective changes.
- Experience is what you get when you don't get what you want.
- You can make excuses or you can achieve your goals, but you can't do both.
- You teach what you need to learn.

Though commonly cited, these memorable phrases are anything but clichés, for they truly capture the essence of transforming challenge into triumph. These four truisms distill the *Don't Die* message that each author in the series captures through his or her personal story. As a Positive Psychology practitioner and Organizational Psychologist who has counseled executives for over 25 years, I serve as the series curator and as your guide as you translate each story into inspiration for your life.

Behavioral science cannot pinpoint how long it takes for an individual to embrace a life change. Some common markers are 36 months for a major change, 12 months for a life adjustment, and 28 days for a new habit. *Don't Die* books tend to capture true stores that, not surprisingly, traverse 36 months from the beginning to end, and concentrate on 12 months when events, through synchronicity, coalesce to evolve to the next level.

To heighten the synchronicity of your life, read the book, live the spirit, and use the journal pages in the back to create your own story of resilience.

Happy reading. Happy writing. Happy singing.

Andrea
10/5/11

This book is the story of a man given up at birth and the story of a man who never gave up.

This is a story of love.

This is a story about doing what you love even when what you are doing is not your first love.

This is a story of love built with synchronicity, forgiveness, miracles, and smiles.

Change Your Awareness and Your Perspective Changes

We don't see things as they are, we see them as we are.

—Anais Nin

Synchronicity

Time moves fast for David Fischer, and he does not waste the time he has. He's a marathon-running, entrepreneurial 30-something New Yorker. He does not spend his time on YouTube. He does not spend his time listening to Frank Sinatra music. He did not know Gary Russo before August 1, 2011.

A couple of days before, he had walked down the street in his New York City neighborhood. He happened to hear a construction worker singing during his lunch break to a small crowd.

He thought he sounded pretty good. Really good, in fact. He asked the guy if he could come back and tape him.

Then, on August 1, David went back with his video camera to tape the 2nd Avenue Subway Sinatra. He uploaded it as his first post to YouTube in five years.

On his way back to work, David called his buddy Danny Gold, a reporter at the *New York Post*. "I just posted a video on YouTube. I've sent you the link. You gotta see this guy. He's great. It would be a great story."

Danny wasn't convinced. There are plenty of people singing on the streets of New York every day, he said. "Yeah," agreed David. "But none of them are employed construction workers devoting their only lunch break to singing to make people smile."

The friend in Danny was amused at David's uncharacteristic enthusiasm, but the reporter in him couldn't see how he could break away from a murder investigation in Brooklyn to check out a singing construction worker in Manhattan.

They hung up. David had given it his best shot, but thought he had failed.

Unbeknownst to David, Danny did what friends do. He listened even when he didn't want to. He begrudgingly went to YouTube and checked out the video. Intrigued, he figured out the location of the job site from the sign for Little Vincent's Pizza in the background of the shot. He left the murder investigation and headed out to find the singer in the hard hat.

The interview was completed before David even knew it was being conducted.

In the early morning of August 2, over half a million copies of the *New York Post* with a large photo of Gary and a headline "2nd Avenue Serenade" hit newsstands across the city. The story ran on the paper's website.[1]

The YouTube hits started pouring in. And so did the offers.

What caused David to return, video camera in hand, to record a guy singing on the street?

Up until that point, David and Gary's interaction was like others that had taken place over the initial days of Gary's noontime concerts. People would pass by. Some would notice him, and a few would stop momentarily and catch a short video on their phones. A few posted those videos on YouTube. None of the posts generated a following. None changed Gary's life.

Until David's on August 1. His action set in motion a living definition of synchronicity.

Synchronicity is the experience of two or more events that are causally unrelated occurring together in a meaningful manner. The unrelated event that made the difference in Gary's case was David's decision to connect with his connections and use them on behalf of a person he had never been connected to before. That's why the real synchronicity transpired after David uploaded the video.

> *Synchronicity is the experience of two or more events that are causally unrelated occurring together in a meaningful manner.*

Synchronicity occurs at the intersection of your **awareness, response, perspective,** and **action**.

Awareness and Response

The slow dance of synchronicity begins the moment you are born. Throughout life, you'll have many partners in this dance. They come in and out on the wings of unrelated events. Yet rarely are you aware that these events could make a difference in your life.

You become aware when you slow your mind enough to think about the events as a coincidence taking place right before your eyes.

When you chose to respond to those thoughts, they carry power beyond your imagination.

This connection may remind you of the Law of Attraction.[2] A bastardized and morphed popular culture version of this theory has been floating around for several years. The incomplete version goes something like this: You have thoughts, and those thoughts become things—good or bad. Net, net your thinking attracts to you good things if you think good thoughts, and bad things if you think bad thoughts. So according to this theory, the mere act of thinking can get you into trouble. Since every individual has an average of 50,000 thoughts a day—most of them unconscious—this version of the Law of Attraction gives people more responsibility for their lives than even the most highly functioning among us can possibly handle!

Richard Rohr has a more useful interpretation of how you might attract situations into your life:

- You create your response to all things that occur.
- Your response is your reality.

◆ Therefore you create your reality . . . or attract what is in your life by how you respond to all things in your life.[3]

Your response can be a mental action, like a decision to see things differently. Since you create that response, you also have the opportunity to alter it. That's how you create your reality.

Your thoughts. Your response. Your reality. Your Law of Attraction.

Cause and effect, means and ends, seed and fruit, cannot be severed; for the effect always blooms in the cause, the end preexists in the means, the fruit in the seed.

—Ralph Waldo Emerson

Perspective

The definition of synchronicity says that the unrelated events "occur together in a meaningful manner." Notice that the definition doesn't specify if the meaning is good, or if the meaning is bad. That's where your perspective comes into play.

Take the perspective of the birth of a child. A joyous occasion, right? Or is it one of those myths we rarely want to call out from under the carpet? The idea that all births are joyous occasions is one of those myths that build a *Don't Die* spirit. More times than we wish to admit, babies come into this world wrapped in a blanket of stressors they had no earthly part in creating.

A baby boy named Gary entered the world in such a way in September, 1960. He was born to a mother of Irish descent whose life stressors led her to give him up for adoption. He was adopted by a mother of Italian descent, whose life stressors led him to the music of Frank Sinatra. She bestowed on him the Italian surname Russo.

Enter synchronicity. Being born, being adopted, growing up as a kid in one family, getting a karaoke machine, marrying, having his own kids, starting businesses, being reunited as an adult with his birth family, losing businesses, finding a job, losing his marriage, and becoming a viral singing phenomenon, are in themselves unrelated events that occurred together over a 50-year time span.

Is Gary a construction worker who sings?

Or a singer who works in construction?

That depends on your perspective.

How he saw himself, and therefore how he ignored or welcomed synchronistic events, depended on his perspective.

His perspective shifted after he began to think of himself differently.

He experienced a series of what are called "perspective-changing events."[4]

Are you laying tracks or building a railroad?

Some stories, like this one, remain so poignant that you hear them again and again in inspirational speeches and self-help books:

> Two railroad employees meet again after first having worked together laying tracks some 30 years before. One employee was still laying tracks. The other former trackman was now the railroad's proud CEO. With equal parts envy and defeat, the trackman questioned the CEO, "How come we started out together laying railroad tracks and after all these years, I am still working outside, fighting nature's elements, doing all the dirty work, and you—you—are the CEO?" With the humility of a seasoned leader, the CEO replied, "You see, 30 years ago you believed your job was to lay railroad tracks. I, on the other hand, believed I was building a railroad."

Perspective. It does change everything.

Same job. Different **perspective** on what they were doing.

Perspective. It does change everything.

Action

You never know when one seemingly unrelated event may become the catalyst that sets off a chain of synchronistic events. Though you may not know for sure when something important will happen, you can always be ready to take action.

In the summer of 2011, Gary Russo was ready.

The steps of being ready to take action and actually taking action connect unrelated events into that powerful chain.

You hold all the potential for great synchronistic events to come together to transform your life.

You hold all the potential for great synchronistic events to come together to transform your life.

You accept the dance partner synchronicity brings you when you take action by stepping into opportunity—even when you don't know in advance the possibility that opportunity may hold.

Experience Is What You Get When You Don't Get What You Want

Experience is not what happens to a man.
It is what a man does with what happens to him.

—Aldous Huxley

Love

Everybody has roots. I have more than most, and they run deep and wide. Like everybody, how I grew up and who raised me made me who I am. Like everybody, there are good parts of my past, and there are parts even I don't like so much. The parts I don't like so much caused me to search for ways to be a better man.

The Internet opens so many windows and doors these days. Without its magic and reach, my audience would still be a handful of 2nd Avenue neighbors. My songs must have meant something to the people who watched me on YouTube.

I've had those Internet moments, too—when some link or email shows up and gives me something I can relate to. There was once a story in my email that reminded me about how I grew up. It went like this:

An Italian mother is giving directions to her grown son, who is coming to visit with his wife.

"You comma to de front door of da apartmenta. Ima inna apartmenta 301. There issa bigga panel at da front door. Witha you elbow, pusha da button 301. I willa buzza you in. Come-a inside, da elevator is on da right. Get in, and witha you elbow, pusha 3. When you getta out, I'mma on da left. Witha you elbow, hit my doorbell."

"Ma, that sounds easy, but, why am I hitting all these buttons with my elbow?

"What??!! . . . you-a gonna comma empa-ty handed?"

From an early age I knew I wanted to make something of myself. It was only when I got older that I realized before that could happen, I had to stop thinking that I was never good enough. I had to stop being afraid I was never *doing* enough. I had to stop thinking that I would never *have* enough.

• •

Aim for success, not perfection. Never give up your right to be wrong, because then you will lose the ability to learn new things and move forward with your life.

—Dr. David M. Burns

There are so many ways a life can be lived. Stories like Gary's can remind you that you can live life with a spirit that won't be killed no matter what life throws your way, or how deep of a rut you feel stuck in. This story can inspire you to live your life with the absolute confidence that you will thrive after adversity, and that you will complete your life with the sense of triumph expressed in this Navajo chant: *When you were born, you cried. And the world rejoiced. Live your life so that when you die, the world cries. And you rejoice.*[5]

People just like you can and do have tough experiences, or what experts call "perspective-changing events." And let's face it: a lot of life is tough. But after a negative incident, not only can you survive, you can also learn to thrive again. Sound like too much of a challenge? It's not: it's entirely possible. The latest Positive Psychology research has scientifically proven that as tough as life is, people do indeed experience this kind of growth. [6]

When you use life's curve balls to create positive energy, you cultivate a *Don't Die* spirit that powers you through moment by moment so that you live your life to the fullest until the very end.

A *Don't Die* spirit emerges from love: love of others, love of self, love of life

This love isn't the "love of your life" love, or "unconditional" love. No, this love is the experience of momentarily increased positive emotions you feel when you invest in the well-being of another, or when your response to a situation matches someone else's as though you are in synchrony. Over time, these moments of love add up to "embodied rapport"—that sense of things just clicking. [7]

To love others, first find that sense of connection within yourself. In other words, love yourself first. That's when you will learn to love life.

Forgiveness

When I started with the Kiewit Company, I knew I was lucky. To have steady work early in my career as an iron worker was great. But to have it with a company like Kiewit was even better. What I had no way of knowing was how much working with and for that company would change my life.

Everyone who sees the story on the Internet about me singing on my lunch break to help smooth over the angry neighbors of a job site thinks I did the company a big favor. That's not even close to the whole story.

Only a few people know the whole truth. The only reason I was on that job site at all was because the company once took a big chance and forgave me for walking off a job and vanishing for over 10 months. I just kinda disappeared. I'm not proud of the way I left.

They didn't have to take me back. I wasn't given my supervisor title again, but I had a job. From the day they took me back, I always looked for ways to make the company proud. I call it the "best worst decision" I ever made.

Forgiveness is not something you think of when you think of a big construction company—or any company for that matter. But their forgiveness years before set the stage for the story of this unbelievable year.

● ●

Did you ever take a class in forgiveness? Probably not, unless you studied theology.

Forgiveness is an internal, psychological shift people who feel they were wronged make for themselves, by themselves.

Do you ever think about companies practicing forgiveness? Sounds like a long shot, doesn't it? Yet forgiveness may well open doors to business success.

Kiewit took a calculated business risk to trust that Gary had made the necessary changes within himself so that he could move beyond the reasons he had walked off the job. In forgiving Gary, the company showed that it supports people who learn from mistakes. It demonstrated that it values the very humanness of its workers. Through this one act, the company communicated that it knows that success comes not from short-term gains and blind application of policies, but from continual learning by people who bring not just their heads, but also their hearts, to work.

But what's most important is not that Kiewit forgave Gary. What's most important is that Gary forgave Gary.

What's most important is that Gary forgave Gary.

When people forgive themselves, they stop beating themselves up over decisions and words they can't take back. They give themselves a second chance. They express love to themselves. They let themselves move into the future with a reinvigorated *Don't Die* spirit.

You Can Make Excuses or You Can Achieve Your Goals, but You Can't Do Both

He that is good for making excuses is seldom good for anything else.

—Benjamin Franklin

The Miracle of Kiewit

I don't know if I will be working for Kiewit forever. I do know that Kiewit has been my greatest teacher in how to "be."

Let me explain. I knew Kiewit was different even before they took me back after my little "best worst thing" vanishing act. I knew it was a great company to work for because it respected you, it offered good benefits, and it didn't just *talk* about you being an owner, they actually *invited* you to be an owner. I knew all of that. Then something happened that made me see that all the things I was doing to try to make my life better were exactly the things they'd been teaching me to do at work in order to do my work better.

The light went on about 12 years into working for them, when I was on my first big railroad project. The company was pushing for greater efficiency, better turnaround times, and more cooperation. All of us supervisors on the job were brought into a meeting. I can't remember who ran the meeting or where it was, but I remember how it felt when I realized the similarity between my own personal development work and what they were teaching us.

They asked us to write down goals. They asked us to look at photos showing what a more efficient operation or success would look like. They asked us to see beyond what we thought we could do. And then they asked us to go to that "beyond" place. I realized these were the lessons they had been teaching me since the day I started. I just never made the connection that doing those same things at home would help me get better results in all areas of my life.

Sure, I'd been reading self-help books. Sure, I'd been going to seminars. And sure as I'm telling you this, I did not see the connection until that day. You can go from seeking to seeker when you stop bouncing from seminar to seminar and you actually set a plan for change and take the risks you need to take without worrying about failing.

There is no explaining it; something just clicked that day.

• •

"There is no explaining it; something just clicked."

Well, actually, there are lots of ways to explain it.

A learning theorist would explain it by describing the tension in the learning process that allows the brain to finally connect disparate learning experiences.

A self-help guru would recite the oft-used maxim, "the teacher will come when the student is ready."

A behavioral scientist might explain the "it" with a discussion on the psychology of achievement.

And all of those explanations would be correct.

The "it" no one theory or explanation can ever adequately explain is the feeling you will experience viscerally in your body when you spontaneously make that connection for yourself.

You Teach What You Need to Learn

We are all teachers; the question is not whether we will teach,
but what.

—Anonymous

Smiles

I like the limelight. I always have.

Being in front of people never bothered me, so when the opportunity came up to share the story that I called "The Miracle of Kiewit," my heart smiled. I would be able to give back the gift I had been given—the gift about setting goals, seeing the bigger picture and the end game, about seeing bigger than you thought you could ever see. I was going to get to teach the guys, my brothers, what I had learned.

When I think about how it felt to prepare for that talk, I can remember being anxious, excited, and scared, all at once. It reminded me of being a kid on Christmas morning. All that anticipation: What presents will I get? Will I get what I asked for? Or will I get more? And of course, some of that fear mixed in: Was I really good enough to get any of the things I asked for?

I knew I had been given the gift of learning for myself. Now, I was getting to give that gift back. My heart was smiling. I was smiling.

• •

To teach is to learn twice.

—Joseph Joubert

The thing about perspective-changing events is that they usually don't announce themselves as such. Plus, change often takes so much time that you don't recognize the long-ago events that started it.

There comes a point when change takes the form of a new learning, a new awareness, a new perspective. This shift happens when you share what you have learned.

Each time you share, you are actually teaching.

Each time you teach, you learn something else you needed to know.

That is why, when you teach, you learn twice.

Teaching is a gift you give not only to others, but also to yourself. You give and you receive, you teach and you learn. You see smiles, and you smile yourself.

When people come into your life for a SEASON . . .
Because your turn has come to share, grow, or learn,
They bring you an experience of peace, or make you laugh.
They may teach you something you have never done.
They usually give you an unbelievable amount of joy.
Believe it! It is real! But, only for a season.

> —Anonymous, as transmitted around the Internet

Reasons and Seasons

The seasons are what a symphony ought to be: four perfect movements in harmony with each other.

—Arthur Rubenstein

Poets and popes and psychologists invoke the seasons to make sense of the world around us.

Life changes as seasons change. And with each season, we, like the farmer, have a job to do in the cultivation of our *Don't Die* spirit.

As summer gave way to fall, Gary began to appreciate the seasonal synchronicity of his story:

A winter to prepare the seed of change

A spring to nurture vulnerable shoots of new life

A summer to work each day to nurture that new life

A fall to harvest the fruit of the year's work

Months combine to create a season. Days combine to make a month. For Gary, just one month—the 31 days of August—added up to one incredible journey. A summer journey that wouldn't have been possible without the winter and spring that came before, and would not be complete without a full fall harvest.

Winter

In the depth of winter I finally learned that there was in me an invincible summer.

—Albert Camus

Cold Winter, Warm Thoughts of Change

I don't think I had ever been so cold on a job site. It was the coldest winter the Northeast had seen in over a decade. I was in Massachusetts, away from home, away from my kids. But I was grateful to have work. I knew many were not as fortunate. I had a job to go to, even if it was cold and far from home. I had a lot of time to think. I was thinking about Tracy telling me two years earlier she was not happy. I was thinking about how hard life had been since we split. I also thought about how much I loved my kids and how lucky I was to be working. Those positive thoughts were all that kept me warm.

Maybe the cold, the separation, and the gratitude all mixed together to help me recognize that the time had come to make some changes in my life. The only way I can explain what I was feeling is to think about seeing those pictures of the effects of the warming at the North Pole. Huge pieces of ice cracking, cracking, cracking, until they just break off and form a whole new iceberg. It was time for me to start breaking down and away from some bad habits. Time for me to form new ways to be me.

Like so many guys, I spent a lot of my years doing what I needed to do. I guess by the time of that Massachusetts job, I had lived enough of those years. Now I wanted to figure out how to do what I *needed* to do, and what I *wanted* to do. What I wanted was to start doing all the creative stuff that had been rolling around in my head for way too long.

One thing I wanted to start doing was singing in public. Another was I wanted to write. I had ideas. I thought about television shows I wanted to write. I thought about movie scripts I wanted to write. I realized what I wanted to be was more creative in general.

● ●

Insanity: doing the same thing over and over again and expecting different results.

—Albert Einstein

No matter how cold your proverbial winter, you can plant seeds of change in your life by changing your thoughts and actions.

Nothing changes in your life until you change something. If you, like Gary, want to form a new way to be you, to change *how* or *who* you are, start thinking of ways to be different. And then *act* differently, too.

Without change from within, you'll get the same results, even if the world around you shifts.

True change from within can translate into goals so powerful that excuses fade in comparison.

Gary and daughters Cara and Amber

Spring

If we had no winter, the spring would not be so pleasant; if we did not sometimes taste of adversity, prosperity would not be so welcome.

—Anne Bradstreet

Out of the Mouths of Babes . . .

Amber asked me, "Dad, can we go white water rafting in the Grand Canyon? Just me and you. It will be fun."

Fun or not, I said no.

I hated, *really* hated, not being able to say yes. Amber had dreams running through her head. I had my bank balance running through mine. Then another thought ran through my head. I remembered a conversation weeks before with my younger daughter, Cara. She's one of those kids who is an old soul in a young body. She's one of my many life teachers. She had wanted to do something, too, and I had said no. The gentle way she looked at me and lowered her voice while she held my eyes in a locked gaze got my attention. "Daddy, you are so cheap."

Cheap? Me? The voice in my head immediately protested. I provide for my family as well as a man can. Given all that had happened in my life and the construction industry, I knew I couldn't say yes. It killed something inside me. I mean it. I felt like a little piece of me was dying just because I couldn't say yes to my girls' dreams.

Then it came to me. What I needed to kill was the way I was thinking. Maybe my girls were telling me that *I* didn't think I had enough. Maybe they were trying to show me how rich I was in all the ways that count, when all I could count was the money in my bank account.

And then I made a decision. I told myself, "I'm not going to keep thinking this way. I'm not going to live this way. This is not the way I want to think about living."

. . . Ideas Spring . . .

The goal of singing in public wasn't just some goal I had thought up out of nowhere because I was stuck in a hotel room during a cold winter. I had had a karaoke machine since I was a kid. And I would sing everywhere I could, much to the embarrassment of my wife and kids.

Goals have lots of pieces, and there are lots of opportunities to either walk toward your goal or pretend you really never set one.

When I first started thinking about how to sing more in public, I didn't think at first about singing on my lunch break.

Instead, I went through some steps that I would have had to do to make any performance a possibility. I had to get equipment. I had to start putting my music together. I had to think about where or how I could really sing more publicly.

Cara calling me cheap actually helped me think of one venue that might work. I loved taking her down to Washington Square Park and watching the street performers. It was something we could do together, and it was free. What if I took my equipment down there and tried joining the street party? No, that felt too intimidating. I'm an outgoing guy who likes to have fun, but the people on the streets of New York can be tough critics. I thought about it, but it didn't feel right.

I knew I had the right idea. I didn't want to kill it, so I had to keep thinking.

. . . and Music Flows

Losing weight probably had as much to do with me coming up with the idea to sing on the job site as anything else.

About the time I started setting goals about being more creative, I also decided I wanted to take better care of myself. To do that, I needed to lose 30 pounds. I'm not the tallest guy in the world, so 30 pounds can make more of a difference on me than on most.

Without really realizing how important it was to my future, I had gone from one lunch break of sodas and sandwiches to a grazing schedule of mostly fruits and nuts. My energy was up. My belief in myself was up, too. I found I enjoyed using my lunch breaks for reading more than for eating. That's when the idea to sing on my lunch breaks really started to come together for me.

I would try to settle in to read on my break, but the noise from the job site was too distracting. There is no such thing as a silent construction site, and there is no such thing as being able to sit and read enjoyably in the middle of one. I knew the tenants in the surrounding blocks had been complaining about the noise, and now I understood why. Of course I also understood that the project was of critical importance to improving the transportation alternatives in that part of the city. So the project had to go on. What could *I* do to make this better? Better for them? Better for me?

That's when it first popped into my head to sing instead of read on my lunch break.

You learn to speak by speaking, to study by studying, to run by running, to work by working; in just the same way, you learn to love by loving.

—Anatole France

Connecting Ideas

From: Gary Russo
Date: Thu, 9 June 2011 19:12:01 +0400
To: Andrea Goeglein
Subject: Glad to reconnect

Hi Andrea,

It was so good to see you the other day. Especially to see Cara and the family having a good time. It really made my heart swell to see you give your time to help my little one get into the scavenger hunt. Time goes too quick. I am very impressed with your site and the work you do. "Dr Success" — I love it. I've been on a path of discovery for the past few years. It must have been the water in Richmond Hill that put us on this path of looking for more in life. LOL Just downloaded Shifting Sands on my Nook. Looking forward to following your success. Stay well and help the world get better. Keep in touch. Love to you and the family. Thanks for cousin Jeannie's number, I'm working 500 ft from her front door.

—Gary

Spring is nature's way of saying, "Let's party!"

—Robin Williams

In spring, you wait impatiently for those first shoots of growth to emerge from the still-cold soil. It takes a lot of time for that seed, underground, to prepare its ascent.

So it is with ideas. Before they come to life in a way that you can see, that you can touch, they germinate inside you.

A lot of time passes between an idea *inspiring* you to take action, the *decision* to take action, and actually *taking action* on (or *executing*) the idea.

Synchronicity is about connecting unrelated people and events. Synchronicity feeds the seed.

> *Synchronicity is about connecting unrelated people and events. Synchronicity feeds the seed.*

For Gary, going to a family party and reconnecting with family members from another time in his life nurtured the seed of his idea. He chose to take action to connect that past to his present, all in service of his future.

Aunt Chris, Gary, Uncle Andy, Cousin Andrea and Cara

Shift Happens

Meeting up with my cousin Andrea after all these years kinda jolted me into a higher gear. I felt the shift inside me, but I still couldn't make things happen. We were working long days and most weekends to keep the 2nd Avenue Subway project on target.

The girls were out of school for the summer and the rhythm of life in the city was changing, but my life still hadn't changed as much as I wanted it to. I wasn't singing in public. That idea had gotten stuck in my head. Time was passing and I was feeling restless. I started to wonder if too much time would pass before I got the chance to live more of my dreams. I was still on my journey of reading, exploring personal development material, and surfing life-success orientated websites, but I didn't feel like it was all going anywhere.

I needed to get my goal out of my head and into the world.

● ●

The best way to make your dreams come true is to wake up.

—Paul Valery

Summary

All summer long, we sang a song . . .

>—From *Summer Wind*,
>>music by Henry Mayer, lyrics by Johnny Mercer
>>As made famous by Frank Sinatra (1966)
>>As performed by Gary Russo, August 1, 2011

Have you ever wondered how much your life could change in 31 days?

Gary Russo was trying to change his life. He didn't set out to do it in 31 days, but all the pieces came together for him during the month of August, 2011.

He started the month being known by many, and loved by a few, as Gary Russo, iron worker, Local 40.

He ended the month being loved for his singing and known by millions as the "2nd Avenue Subway Sinatra."

Sure, Gary had done his work well before July turned to August. He had laid the groundwork by using events in his life to change his perspective.

Being forgiven by Kiewit

Connecting learning at work with his own search for more

Making a commitment to himself and losing weight

Hearing his daughter's comments about money

All those events came together so that, over the 31 days of August, a handful of people—some he had known for years, and others he had never met—could usher in synchronicity on the wings of what may otherwise have been unrelated events that may have been meaningless if he hadn't first changed his perspective.

"Dan, I think at lunch time, I'm gonna start singin'."
There. I had said it.

At our usual happy hour, I had finally mustered up the courage to tell my site boss Dan what had been on my mind for a while.

Dan tilted his head in that way that said he wasn't sure he had heard right.

Dan composed himself and said, "Sing?"

I said, "Yeah, I have this little machine, and I have some music. I think I just wanna sing for the neighbors during lunch."

I don't think he thought I was serious. But he just smiled a half smile and said, "Well, okay."

That brief exchange made me take the next step toward a goal I'd formed so long ago. OK, I never wrote a goal or said, "I want to sing on the streets of New York City during my lunch hour." My goal was to sing. My goal was to make other people smile. My goal was to sing and make other people smile because I knew that would make *me* smile.

I knew Dan had seen me perform a number maybe once or twice at some company event. Over the years I had grabbed any chance to sing when people were around. Even so, I don't think Dan thought I was serious. Dan knew I liked to have a good time. He kinda believed me, but not really. If I'm to be truthful, I kinda believed me, but not really.

I kinda believed me, but not really.

Then I hesitated. The voice in my head was doing a lot of talking and not much singing. My head was flooded with all the reasons why my idea wouldn't work. How was I going to get the equipment to the site? Where would I put it while I worked? Why did I ever say anything to Dan?!

Now I was coming to see that making that first announcement was the easy part. The real work was about to begin.

I started to get a second dose of courage. I thought back to those cold days on the job site in Massachusetts when I started thinking about the things I still wanted to achieve. It was all about getting the creative stuff out of my head and into the world. I had come up with the idea of singing on the site to help the neighbors and, if truth be told, me, deal with the noise.

I made the idea real by saying it to Dan. I had no backdoor escape route now. I had to prove to Dan and myself that I would really do it. That's where I found the courage. I was really asking *me* to believe in *me*.

That's the cool thing about telling other people the ideas you have bouncing around in your head. You think it's about telling them, but you're really just challenging yourself.

● ●

You Can Make Excuses or You Can Achieve Your Goals, but You Can't Do Both

Day 1
Monday, August 1, 2011

We worked that last weekend in July. I started experimenting with singing that Friday. The first day had gone okay. There I was, on a street in New York, in my work clothes, standing there with the karaoke, the hard hat, and the little sign, crooning away. Some people stared as they walked by, some didn't even notice. A few actually stopped and I got to see their faces as the words to whatever song I was singing connected to their lives. More people probably walked passed that day than actually stopped, but I quickly learned how few smiles it takes to get the encouragement to keep going.

People with their fancy phones record their own experience as they walk down the street these days. When I put myself out there, I ended up being part of their experience. Some guy even asked if he could come back and tape me.

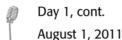

Day 1, cont.
August 1, 2011

The noontime concerts, as I began to call them, almost didn't happen at all. I had found the courage to stand on the street and sing. Then I had to see if I could sustain them through all the initial setbacks. On Sunday, when I tried to start my concert, my iPod failed and I had to scrap my plans for that day. I was quickly learning that my desire to sing and see people smile was going to take as much perseverance as courage and talent.

A job site is run on a tight schedule. That's why I knew lunch would always be from 12 to 12:30 and could schedule concerts. On Monday, August 1, though, the schedule got mixed up. A delivery truck came late and we had to get it unloaded before we could break for lunch. We were all working as hard and as fast as possible, but the noon hour arrived and we weren't done. I started to feel disappointed. I knew my chance to sing that day was slipping away.

When we finished about ten minutes later, I started debating with myself. Should I go do a concert in the 20 minutes I have left? Should I skip today? Will it really matter? And in a flash, I just heard myself answer, *you must do it*.

As I scrambled to get everything in place, I was feeling better and better. By the time I began to sing *Summer Wind*, I was in a groove. I felt good. Really good.

I looked out into the audience and saw that the guy who had stopped by on Saturday had actually come back with his video camera.

As I ended the song, I smiled. It was another sweltering New York City August afternoon, but through the heat and the sweat, I felt so much gratitude. I paused and greeted everyone with a hello and as I did, the guy who had come back with his camera started to ask me questions.

"Hey, Gary, say your name."

"Hi, I'm Gary Russo, from Queens."

With the video still rolling, the guy beckoned me to give more, "Where you workin'?"

Obligingly, and still smiling, I replied, "Workin' here on the 2nd Avenue Subway and we're, ah, tryin' to give back a little bit. Ya know, lunchtime."

Finally satisfied the guy tossed out, "Thank you."

I fumbled. I could sense something big had just happened, but I had no idea what it was, so I just tossed back the gift, "Thank you."

It wasn't until later that day when I saw the video on YouTube that I heard how he had wrapped up the interview.

"This is Fish. This is Gary. Second Avenue Subwaaaaay. In New York City. Construction.

See yah."

• •

http://youtu.be/yoOwCSgvNs0

50 years of living

Two minutes and 30 seconds of video

Life as Gary Russo knew it changes in the closing dialogue with an amateur videographer at a major New York City subway construction site

Gary and David Fischer

Good Morning, Synchronicity!

Day 2
Tuesday, August 2, 2011

When David Fischer wrapped up that video, I had no way of knowing how prophetic his "see yah" sign-off was: people really would see me after that.

I woke up on August 2 ready to start the day like any other work day. Then I saw something I never dreamed of, conceived of, or wrote a goal about: my picture in the *New York Post* and an article about my noontime concerts. Sure, the reporter had come the day before and talked to me. But I figured it'd be a little mention somewhere—not a long article with a big picture.

Today's noontime concert had a very different feel. There were cameras, there were media people. There was this very nice young lady who approached me and asked if I wanted to be on *Good Morning America*!

Good Morning America! What could I say but, "Sure I would." I gave her my phone number and thought it was all kinda funny.

The funny stuff, though, is what happened all afternoon. The *Today* show, The *Early Show* . . . all kinds of media calls to the union hall trying to find me. Media calls to the company trying to find me.

And then came the lesson in integrity.

• •

Confidence is what you have before you understand the problem.

—Woody Allen

The Value of Your Word

Day 3
Wednesday, August 3, 2011

I've been a lot of things in 50 years. I've owned and run video stores, a deli, a café, had a home remodeling business, and I've been a proud iron worker for the last 15 years. What I'd never been was an Internet singing sensation. I'd never thought I'd be approached by—let alone fought over by—the biggest morning shows in the world.

I did what I always do when something seems right. I said yes. I gave my word to the producer from *Good Morning America* because she was the first to ask, I was honored, and she came to me in person.

So when producers from the other shows started asking why I would go with *GMA* and not their higher rated shows, I had no answer other than "I gave my word." The producer of another show didn't seem to understand where I was coming from. But I was quickly coming to understand what instant fame can do to you if you let it. It can teach you to sell out to the highest bidder. It can have you thinking thoughts you don't feel good about thinking—like, "If I go back on my word, I bet I could make more money."

Having lived through my "best worst decision" a few years earlier, I had learned. Integrity is the only right answer.

• •

Hitting Walls and Making the Right Decisions

Day 7
Sunday, August 7, 2011

Seven days in I hit the wall. I had a tough night's sleep, or should I say I had a tough night because I couldn't sleep. With all that had happened since the appearance on *Good Morning America*—the clip on *World News Tonight*, the record promoter coming from England, all the Internet coverage, getting ready to do *Access Hollywood* live in Rockefeller Plaza —I panicked. I was stuck. I kept thinking about all of my goals and dreams and why I even cared.

I cared because I wanted to create a better life for my kids. Now that all this had happened, even though I never expected it, I wanted to make sure I did the right thing for them. And I didn't want to sell out just for money. Never was I doing this for the money.

I had to get a hold of myself. Monday I would be doing the live show with Billy Bush for *Access Hollywood*. I was so excited. I know I kept saying I didn't believe all this, but I really didn't believe it all. Then the money thoughts started to creep into my dreams and I started thinking, "Should I try to get sponsorships from the manufacturers of the work shirt or boots I wear?" "Am I missing an opportunity to provide for my family?"

I didn't want people to think I was doing all this for the money. I wanted to be fair and I didn't want to appear desperate. And I wanted to make the right decisions.

So much of personal development and growth comes down to the decisions you make when you hit a wall. Do you spend your time feeling bad for yourself, or do you invest your time in continuing to build toward your dreams?

Learn to manage your expectations. Instead of focusing on what is most likely NOT going to happen today, use your energy to TAKE ACTION on those things that possibly *can* happen.

When you manage your expectations, you let yourself soak in the joy of what is actually happening around you. One of the challenges of having big dreams is that you can get so hung up on the dream that you don't appreciate all the good that comes to you in the meantime.

When you can appreciate what shows up between here and your dreams, you allow synchronicity to connect the pieces of your life into an enjoyable whole. Maintaining your awareness of little victories keeps you going on the way to your big dreams.

Want to lose 20 lbs? Celebrate that you lost one of them this week.

Want to sing to large crowds of adoring fans? Start singing to a few angry neighbors.

I have learned this at least by my experiment: that if one advances confidently in the direction of his dreams, and endeavors to live the life which he has imagined, he will meet with a success unexpected in common hours.

—Henry David Thoreau

You Teach What You Need to Learn

Day 11

August 11, 2011

From: Roger

Date: Thu, 11 Aug 2011 2:57:38 -0800

To: Gary Russo

Subject: Dreams of singing standards for a lifetime.

Hello Gary,

I just happened to read an email from my sister that featured your "Summer Wind" version of the famous Sinatra song!

Wow! Excellent!

I think what happened to me tonight was that I finally had that catalyst moment!

I listened to you talk about being fifty, following your dreams and how, sometimes, people don't see them until later in life.

Deep inside I felt an urge to sing since I was very young. I knew that I could but a fear that no one else would accept it kept me from following my dream...along with other factors such as wanting to do what was right in life.

I spent many years searching for answers in life. I studied Theology

---

for over 20 years. I studied business, economics and people on my own, still searching for truth. But I also did something else. I studied music. I studied voice. I sang and sang and sang.

My vocal instructor said that she felt that I had the most potential as a soloist in all of our choir...a two hundred person choir.

When she said it I was shocked! I did not see it myself!

Today, I am 55 years of age and I finally see what she and many others were telling me over the years.

Tonight, your singing and your message inspired me to continue toward the threshold I have been moving toward for so many years.

Would you care to hear some samples of my singing? Karaoke background is my method, as is yours right now. But perhaps, in time, we may both be in front of a twenty piece swing band!

Thank you for your inspiration! You are on your way, brother!

Sincerely,

Roger _____

Seattle, Washington

Live as if you were to die tomorrow. Learn as if you were to live forever.

—Gandhi

Change Your Awareness and
Your Perspective Changes

Day 12

Friday, August 12, 2011

——-Original Message——-

From: Damian _____;

Date: Fri, 12 Aug 2011 07:59:55

To: Gary Russo

Subject: Re: Universal Music Negotiations

G

We have some good interest from Universal Music in the UK. I am speaking to them later.

I will let you know how things progress. Also planning to approach the other labels shortly.

D

================================

From: Gary Russo

Date: Fri, 12 Aug 2011 09:08:14

To: Damian _____; Jennifer _____

Subject: Re: Universal Music Negotiations

Good morning to all.

Thank you all for all the hours of hard work that has gone on on my behalf. Just want to thank you so much. Also like to share some things I understand about this crazy business and the way networks and TV work.

The hard hat and the Sinatra voice has been told. It's a great story and will always be there. What has happened is that people are trying to find me and thank me for making them smile for the first time in a long time. People are sharing their dreams with me. They just want me to hug them and tell them to follow their hearts. People young and old see hope where they thought it was gone—they want to lose weight, be nicer, sing, paint, write and smile more. And this is global. THIS is the REAL story here and I am most proud of this.

I have some 85 year old bobby sockers wanting to get out at 12 noon to smile again and feel young and alive. A 12 year old girl who made me a promise to go for her dreams. Me, Gary Russo from Queens. They want me to encourage them. This is so powerful.

I will do all I can for all of you to make all of our dreams come to pass. I'm so fine and well that it hurts. Lol. This is amazing. Just want to let you all know where I'm at. I hope all of you are having as much fun as I am.

Love to you all   —G

Day-old Bread

Day 14

Sunday, August 14, 2011

How is it possible that I can be feeling like day-old bread—before I even got to put the dough in the oven?

Sure, there was a deluge of activity. I could see the momentum building before me. I could feel the response at every noontime performance, and yet the doubts started creeping in as fast as the clicks on YouTube.

"He's good, but what he sings has been done before."

"He's good, but so are a lot of people. It has no legs."

"He's a fad. We can't see how it would build."

They couldn't see how it would build, and I had to keep seeing only what could be built. It wasn't easy and it didn't feel good, but I wasn't going to let anything stand in the way of what I knew, *really* knew, was possible.

So yesterday I decided to call my cousin Andrea to muster up some support and get re-grounded.

Wouldn't you know it, she wasn't available. I left a message which started with,

"Hey cuz, they think I'm day-old bread . . . "

I finished the message. I was tired. I was feeling beat so I headed to bed. It was Sunday, August 14. It had been less than 20 days since I told Dan I was going to start using my lunch hours to sing.

• •

Day 15
Monday, August 15, 2011

Today, the clouds parted in New York—both literally and figuratively—and things began to happen.

● ●

When the Experience You Get . . .

30-minute lunch break from 12:00 to 12:30 P.M. Monday;
Gary sings

21:58 hours later an email arrives and he's at work

5:17 hours pass before he can respond to the offer of his
dreams

. . . Is Experience Transformed

Day 16

Tuesday, August 16, 2011

——-Original Message——-
From: Jennifer _____
Date: Tue, 16 Aug 2011 12:51:58 -0400
To: Gary Russo, Damian _____, Josh _____
Subject: Inside Edition

Hi Gary,

Inside Edition has arranged for you to perform at the famed Blue
Note Jazz Club in New York. Can you please tell me if you would be
available this Thursday evening to perform and tape the segment?

We are waiting for an exact time, but you would need to arrive a little
before 7:00 p.m. Are you able to get off work early to get home,
shower, dress and get over to West 3rd Street?

If not, please let me know asap so I can work with the producer on
an alternative date.

Thanks, Jennie
===============================
From: Gary Russo
Date: Tue, 16 Aug 2011 17:17:00 +0000
To: Jennifer _____
Subject: Re: Inside Edition

Omg. I will be there with bells on. Anytime they need me NP.
Gary

The Gift of Being Present

Day 22

August 22, 2011

From: Gary Russo
Date: Mon, 22 Aug 2011 18:42:09 +0900
To: Andrea Goeglein
Subject: Coming to Vegas!

Hi Cuz,

I'm coming to Las Vegas! I just wanted to let you know what's going on. The head of my Union asked me to come to a convention. He was at a meeting and my name came up. This is such a good thing. They want me to sing and tell my story. I think this positive message has reached my fellow union family. I'm so proud to do this on a national level, and would love to share on the local level, too.

He called yesterday morning, but I couldn't get to the computer until now. We were really crunched at the site yesterday working towards a goal, AND WE MADE IT!!! Was one of those days when nothing was going right. We pushed and pushed and it seemed like the harder we pushed one way the more we were thrown back in the opposite direction. We joked that we didn't know if we were building a subway or if a train was headed straight toward us!!! Then things finally began to work and we made the goal for the day. It was a Kiewit miracle!!!!!

G

PS—I'll call you when I know more details about Vegas. Hope you're around to see me and meet up.

981,000 views of David Fischer's August 1 post on YouTube

An invitation to speak at North American Iron Workers/ Impact Labor Management Conference

Why, after generating close to 1 million YouTube hits, after appearing on *Good Morning America*, after presenting on the topic of goal setting within his company, would Gary Russo be surprised by the invitation to speak at one of his industry's national conventions?

The sense of awe and innocence in his reaction revealed that he still didn't believe what had happened over the last few weeks and its potential implication to his life calling.

He was, as trite as it sounds, walking on the air of his new-found fame. Yet he also remained truly grounded, connected to his reality and his "brothers" at work. What was he really excited about? The goal he and the guys hit the day before on the construction site.

When you remain present to the goal at hand, you become ready to receive a powerful gift. The gift is the presence to achieve your dreams.

There is no labor a person does that is undignified,
if they do it right.

—Bill Cosby

31 Days from Wandering to Wonder

From: Lily _____
Date: Thu, September 01, 2011 5:40
To: Gary Russo
Subject: Thank you

Hi - just a note to let you know how terrific and emotional it was this morning. Am going to miss you soooooo much. The rose is beautiful, what a nice idea. The Japanese photographer told me that you are the most popular singer in Japan. Can you imagine that? The whole situation is an unimaginable dream for you and you sure deserve it.

Love, Lily

When you can maintain continual awareness of where you are and hold onto the vision of where you want to go, you transform your life from wandering to wonder.

- ◆ 30 years of work and $700 in the bank
- ◆ 30 years of singing to anyone who would listen and no way to turn the passion into a profession
- ◆ 30 minutes during lunch breaks to help transform angry neighbors into smiling supporters
- ◆ 1,005,417 hits on YouTube
- ◆ Countless people wondering if they will be the next to achieve their dreams

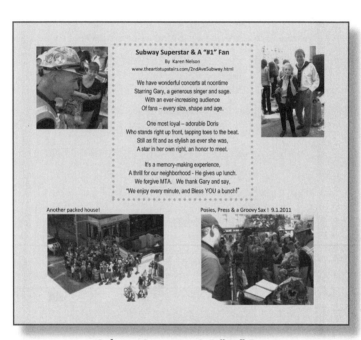

Subway Superstar & A "#1" Fan
By Karen Nelson
www.theartistupstairs.com/2ndAveSubway.html

We have wonderful concerts at noontime
Starring Gary, a generous singer and sage.
With an ever-increasing audience
Of fans – every size, shape and age.

One most loyal – adorable Doris
Who stands right up front, tapping toes to the beat.
Still as fit and as stylish as ever she was,
A star in her own right, an honor to meet.

It's a memory-making experience,
A thrill for our neighborhood - He gives up lunch.
We forgive MTA. We thank Gary and say,
"We enjoy every minute, and Bless YOU a bunch!"

Another packed house!

Posies, Press & a Groovy Sax ! 9.1.2011

Subway Superstar & A "#1" Fan

Blog post by Karen Nelson, September 1, 2011[8]

www.theartistupstairs.com/2ndAveSubway.html

Harvest

"For the rest of my life, I will never forget the faces of the people here."

—Gary Russo, as quoted in
the *Daily News*, 09/02/2011

The Power of a Smile

Sometimes your joy is the source of your smile, but sometimes your smile can be the source of your joy.

—Thich Nhat Hanh

Were people drawn to helping Gary Russo because of Gary's singing, or because Gary smiled as he sang and spoke with others?

When you smile:

People are more willing to help you.
You are more willing to help others.[9]
You create a positive change in your body and mind.
And you create positive change in the world.

Brooke didn't choose to come see me. She had been brought in her stroller. She was there for some of the first noontime concerts, but we didn't speak, so I didn't know who she was. I sang, she smiled. We talked with our eyes and through our hearts.

Her adult caregiver told me she was staying at the Ronald McDonald House nearby.

When I got a request a few days later to sing *New York, New York* for Brooke, she wasn't there. Her Mom had come by to make the request and record the song. I can't tell you how incredible that felt.

I didn't see Brooke again until the last official day of my noontime concerts. She gave me a bracelet, I gave her a rose. Her mom gave me a gift I will cherish for the rest of my life when she told a *Daily News* reporter on September 2:

Brooke gave me a bracelet, I gave her a rose.

"Russo has cheered up Brooke's darkest days. She lights up. She likes to dance to his music. It's an emotional roller coaster every day, but to have something make your day better is just phenomenal."

● ●

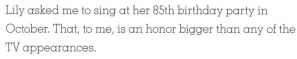

Lily asked me to sing at her 85th birthday party in October. That, to me, is an honor bigger than any of the TV appearances.

Lily had been there since the first noontime concert. She was one of the neighbors I had hoped to make happy by playing music so they would forget about all the construction noise. I sang for the "Lily's" of the neighborhood. The songs I sang were her songs, from her era. Lily had accepted me from the start. What's more important is that she has understood and accepted my gesture of goodwill. She was one of the first to want her picture taken

Lily asked me to sing at her 85th birthday party.

with me. She was the first to suggest I could sing someplace other than on the street during my lunch break.

She had quickly appointed herself my *de facto* music director. She took me to task, saying, "Well you know, why don't you mix it up a bit? How about some new material? You know you can't keep playin' the same song."

Before anyone else, before the videos and the papers and the shows, she had believed in me enough to want to make me better. And now I would be able to return the favor. To believe in her, celebrating another year in her long life.

● ●

———Original Message———
From: Corey _____
Date: Tue, 20 Sep 2011 12:25:09 PM EDT
To: Damian _____;
Subject: Gary Russo as the "Start Line Sinatra"

Hey Damian,
We'd like to have Gary sing "New York, New York" at the start
of the race on Sunday morning, but we'd also like him to be
a part of our opening night celebration (a first this year) in
Central Park to lead thousands of international runners (many
a part of our Parade of Nations) in a "warm-up" singalong of
the same song. How is he with "working the crowd"?
Corey
================================
From: Damian _____;
Date: Tue, 20 Sep 2011 12:34:03 PM EDT
To: Gary Russo
Subject: Fwd: Gary Russo as the "Start Line Sinatra"

WOW!

I'll sort contracts etc...

D

O n the eve of the autumn equinox, when the sun signals the arrival of harvest time, Gary's dream comes to fruition in the form of an email offering a chance greater than anything he had ever imagined: singing at the New York City Marathon.

This wouldn't just be a huge live audience. It would be 45,000 people who were on the threshold of achieving or repeating their own life dreams.

And the organizers wanted Gary to lead them all—including some of the world's most accomplished athletes—in a song.

The moment I read that email, I knew, *really knew*, that although I couldn't even begin to know the future, I knew, *really knew*, I would never die with my song unsung.

I will live teaching others to sing with me.

That makes my heart smile.

● ●

Come walk with me . . .

—From *Summer Wind*, music by Henry Mayer,
lyrics by Johnny Mercer
As made famous by Frank Sinatra (1966)
As performed by Gary Russo, August 1, 2011

Harvesting Your Goals

Everyone goes through seasons in life. Everyone experiences synchronicity in life. Everyone has perspective-changing events in life. Everyone has life goals.

Not everyone takes action to harvest the experiences of the seasons of life in order to enjoy their bounty. To take action means making a choice for change, just as Gary did in the recent winter of his life.

Only those who sow seeds of change can hope to grow and reap a harvest. Use the prompts and pages here to consider your goals, plant your seeds, nurture your dreams, and reap your harvest.

If you prefer not to write in this book, perhaps because you want to pass it on to someone else, you can download worksheets with these questions at http://www.servingsuccess.com.

Change your awareness and

What miracles have I experienced in my life?
What other perspective-changing events have I experienced?

_____

_____

_____

_____

_____

_____

_____

_____

_____

_____

_____

_____

_____

_____

_____

your perspective changes.

What synchronistic events have come into my awareness?

_____

_____

_____

_____

_____

_____

_____

_____

_____

_____

_____

_____

_____

_____

_____

_____

Experience is what you get when

What "best worst decision" have I ever made?

_____

_____

_____

_____

_____

_____

_____

_____

_____

_____

_____

_____

_____

_____

_____

you don't get what you want.

If experience is "what you get when you did not
get what you wanted," what do I want?

_____

_____

_____

_____

_____

_____

_____

_____

_____

_____

_____

_____

_____

_____

You can make excuses or you can achieve

What "song" do I have in my life that I am not singing?
What makes me smile so much that I want to do it in my life?

_____

_____

_____

_____

_____

_____

_____

_____

_____

_____

_____

_____

_____

_____

_____

your goals, but you can't do both.

How could my life change in 31 days?

_____

_____

_____

_____

_____

_____

_____

_____

_____

_____

_____

_____

_____

_____

_____

_____

_____

You teach what

What lesson have I been taught that I need to learn again now?

you need to learn.

Who makes me smile? Who have I made smile?

_____

_____

_____

_____

_____

_____

_____

_____

_____

_____

_____

_____

_____

_____

_____

Quotations

We are seasoned in each other's lives, our joys and sorrows woven into the tapestry of shared history.

—Linda Ellerbee

The world needs dreamers, the world needs doers. But most of all, the world needs dreamers who do.

—Sara Ban Breathnach

We don't see things as they are, we see them as we are.

—Anais Nin

Cause and effect, means and ends, seed and fruit, cannot be severed; for the effect always blooms in the cause, the end preexists in the means, the fruit in the seed.

—Ralph Waldo Emerson

Experience is not what happens to a man. It is what a man does with what happens to him.

—Aldous Huxley

Aim for success, not perfection. Never give up your right to be wrong, because then you will lose the ability to learn new things and move forward with your life.

—Dr. David M. Burns

When you were born, you cried. And the world rejoiced.
Live your life so that when you die, the world cries. And you rejoice.

—Navajo Chant

He that is good for making excuses is seldom good for anything else.

—Benjamin Franklin

We are all teachers; the question is not whether we will teach, but what.

—Anonymous

To teach is to learn twice.

—Joseph Joubert

The seasons are what a symphony ought to be: four perfect movements in harmony with each other.

—Arthur Rubenstein

In the depth of winter I finally learned that there was in me an invincible summer.

—Albert Camus

Insanity: doing the same thing over and over again and expecting different results.

—Albert Einstein

If we had no winter, the spring would not be so pleasant; if we did not sometimes taste of adversity, prosperity would not be so welcome.

—Anne Bradstreet

You learn to speak by speaking, to study by studying, to run by running, to work by working; in just the same way, you learn to love by loving.

—Anatole France

Spring is nature's way of saying, "Let's party!"

—Robin Williams

The best way to make your dreams come true is to wake up.

—Paul Valery

Confidence is what you have before you understand the problem.

—Woody Allen

I have learned this at least by my experiment: that if one advances confidently in the direction of his dreams, and endeavors to live the life which he has imagined, he will meet with a success unexpected in common hours.

—Henry David Thoreau

Live as if you were to die tomorrow. Learn as if you were to live forever.

—Gandhi

There is no labor a person does that is undignified, if they do it right.

—Bill Cosby

Sometimes your joy is the source of your smile, but sometimes your smile can be the source of your joy.

—Thich Nhat Hanh

Notes

1. Jennifer Fermino shared the byline with Danny Gold.

2. The Law of Attraction as first conceptualized in the mid-1800's by Andrew Jackson Davis described Davis' understanding of the soul's journey after death. See Andrew Jackson Davis, *The Great Harmonia*, Vol. IV, *The Reformer* (New York: Redfield, Fowler & Wells, 1853), pp. 40–41. For a contemporary analysis of Davis' writing, please refer to Mitch Horowitz's *Occult America*, Chapter 4, "The Science of Right Thinking" (New York: Bantam Books, 2010).

3. Richard Rohr, *The Naked Now* (New York: The Crossroad Publishing Company, 2009), p. 160.

4. The phrase "perspective-changing events" first appeared in Andrea Goeglein's *Don't Die with Vacation Time on the Books* (Sevierville, Tenn., Insight Publishing Co., 2011).

5. Barbara McAfee, author of *Full Voice* (San Francisco: Berrett-Koehler, 2011), teaches this chant to open inspirational workshops.

6. In Positive Psychology, the ability to thrive after adversity is call "post traumatic growth." This science describes how, even and especially after life-altering events, people can

and do reach a new plateau of well-being. In one thirty-day period, 1700 people took a questionnaire examining the worst things that can happen in a person's life. The traumatic events included torture, grave illness, death of a child, rape, and imprisonment. The finding: "individuals who'd experienced one awful event had more intense strengths (and therefore higher well-being) than individuals who had none. Individuals who'd been through two awful events were stronger than individuals who had one, and individuals who had three—raped, tortured, and held captive for example— were stronger than those who had two." Martin Seligman, *Flourish: A Visionary New Understanding of Happiness and Well-being* (New York: Free Press, A Division of Simon & Schuster, Inc., 2011), p. 160.

7. Barbara Fredrickson, in progress, July, 2011. Definition of love from a slide at Second International Positive Psychology Association meeting: "Love is an interpersonally situated and socially shared experience of one or more positive emotions marked by momentary increases in: 1) investment in the well-being of the other; 2) biobehavioral synchrony; 3) mutually responsive action tendencies; which, over time, build embodied rapport (e.g., we really "clicked").

8. Karen Nelson, September 1, 2011, www.theartistupstairs.com/2ndAveSubway.html

9. Nicolas Gueguen and Marie-Agnes De Gail, "The Effects of Smiling on Helping Behavior: Smiling and Good Samaritan Behavior," *Communication Reports*, 16 (2003), pp. 133–140.

The *Crooked Road of Success*® and the *Don't Die*® Book Series

The Crooked Road of Success is paved with books.

What better way to traverse the potholes and curves of life success than to use the advice offered in books? The *Don't Die* series is the first of an evolving collection of personal development products designed to help you achieve your goals no matter what life throws your way. Each *Don't Die* book offers guidance for developing a personal roadmap of life success.

Join Dr. Success (aka Dr. Andrea Goeglein) as she curates real stories of life journeys into action plans for your personal growth. One book might touch on psychological and spiritual transformation, one on transforming your life into a positive force, and another on the mystery of money and happiness.

Don't Die books are about living life with a spirit that won't be killed no matter what life throws your way. A *Don't Die* spirit is the positive energy you create from not only surviving troubling or traumatic life events, but striving to live well again.

The stories told in each book are constructed around four well-known personal development adages:

- ◆ Change your awareness and your perspective changes.
- ◆ You teach what you need to learn.

- ◆ Experience is what you get when you don't get what you want.

- ◆ You can make excuses or you can achieve your goals, but you can't do both.

Don't Die books form a "small books, big impact" series: small size so that you can read one in 45 minutes. Big impact because that brevity gives you time to consider your real-life *Don't Die* story by working through the exercises in the last section of each book.

Inspiration plus action: that's what *Don't Die* books deliver.

SERVINGSUCCESS®

Your Awareness Starts Here

Everything DiSC® Profile

◆ 10 Minutes of Your Time

◆ 20+ Pages of Information about You

◆ A Great Place for a Lifetime of Learning to Begin

The Everything DiSC® Workplace™ Profile is perfect for every adult use! Don't be put off by the word "workplace."—How you behave at work represents how you behave in your daily life.

The Everything DiSC® Workplace™ is a behavioral instrument that allows you to learn about you. This online version gives you immediate delivery of your profile for a minimal investment of your time and money.

Bonus: Free Comparison Reports!

Now, you can get an easy to read and apply road map for *every* meaningful relationship journey in your life. When someone in your life also invests in a DiSC® profile, you both get a free report comparing your individual styles so that you can create the greatest possible relationship.

For Corporate Clients Only

Inscape Publishing launched the ultimate training department resource with the Everything DiSC® Workplace™ Facilitation Program. This is what one client had to say after just one session using the Facilitation Program:

> *"It went so great! . . . It could not have gone better! . . . ahhhh, what you can do with the right materials!"*
>
> —Shawna Gearhart, *Director of Training, Development & New Store Openings, Bubba Gump Shrimp Company*

And this is what a **CEO candidate** for a **large corporation** said when asked how he managed to be so successful merging so many corporate cultures during his outstanding career. He responded:

> *"I was fortunate as a young man to be introduced to a behavioral profile, DiSC®, and I have used it in every company I have ever led."*

If you would like to learn how your company can enjoy this kind of experience when delivering a team building training, call Dr. Goeglein direct at 1-866-975-3777.

To purchase your individual report today, go to:
http://www.servingsuccess.com/storeandmore.php

About the Authors

Gary Russo

A born entertainer with a *Don't Die* spirit, Gary Russo stepped onto the main stage of his life through a series of synchronistic events in August, 2011. Before winning the hearts of millions of fans around the world as the "2nd Avenue Subway Sinatra," Gary worked in construction, owned his own businesses, and invested in real estate. Gary sees those roles as his attempts to please others by living their definition of success instead of entertaining and pursuing his own.

Since becoming an Internet sensation after the simple gesture of singing during his lunch break, Gary has shared his song and live-your-dreams message through a variety of media outlets, including National Public Radio, *Good Morning America*, *Access Hollywood*, *Fox and Friends*, *World News Tonight with Brian Williams*, the *Rachael Ray Show*, and *Inside Edition*. He has performed at New York's premier venues including the famous Blue Note Jazz Club, Rockefeller Center, the city's Columbus Day parade, and the ING New York City Marathon.

A life-long New Yorker, Gary and his family live in Queens.

Connect with Gary at www.garyrussosite.com or follow him on twitter (garyrusso1).

Andrea T. Goeglien, PhD

Dr. Goeglein is an expert in the application of Positive Psychology to daily life, goal attainment, and overall life success. She earned her doctorate degree in organizational psychology after achieving significant success in business endeavors that included owning a hotel. Now she is devoted to bringing the tenets of Positive Psychology to life for her clients and audiences.

Guided by the principles of love, learning, and prosperity, Dr. Goeglein has been a counselor and personal mentor to the CEOs of privately held companies. She has capitalized on her talents as a dynamic national speaker, major event organizer, community activist, author, and business consultant to build an international portfolio of services. She offers inspirational learning experiences which include invitation-only entrepreneurial success groups, personal executive mentoring, executive women's telegroups, teleclasses, teleseminars, day-long gatherings, video sharing, and books.

A much sought-after media personality known as Dr. Success, Andrea frequently appears as an expert guest on KAZ-TV's *AM Arizona*; she has also appeared on the *Rachael Ray Show* and on major radio networks across the nation. Her interviews, writing, and sightings can be viewed at:

www.YouTube.com/user/ServingSuccess

www.ServingSuccess.com and www.DontDieBooks.com

www.Facebook.com/DrSuccessPhD

To find out how you or your organization can work with Dr. Goeglein, contact DrSuccess@ServingSuccess.com or call 1-866-975-3777.

Create your own *Don't Die* Spirit Living Library

Pass this book on to someone else and encourage
them to do the same when they have finished reading it.

Name of Giver	Date	Gifted to